Title: Python Mastery

Title: Python Mastery

Subtitle: The Complete Guide to Programming with Python from Beginner to Expert.

1: Introduction to Python: Installation and Setup
2: Basic Programming Concepts: Variables, Data Types, and Operators
3: Control Flow and Functions: Conditional Statements and Loops
4: Data Structures: Lists, Tuples, Sets, and Dictionaries
5: Input and Output: Reading and

Python is one of the most popular programming languages in the world. It's a versatile, easy-to-learn, and powerful language that can be used for a variety of tasks, from building web applications to analyzing data to training machine learning models. Python is known for its simplicity, readability, and extensive libraries, which makes it a popular choice for beginners and experts alike.

If you're new to programming or want to learn Python, "Python Mastery: The Complete Guide to Programming with Python" is the perfect resource for you. This comprehensive guide is designed to take you from the basics of Python programming all the way to expert-level proficiency. With clear explanations, real-world examples, and hands-on exercises, you'll learn how to write efficient, maintainable, and scalable code that can handle any task.

The book begins with an introduction to Python, its history, and its applications. You'll learn about the different versions of Python and how to install Python on your computer. The book then moves on to the basics of programming, covering topics such as variables, data types, control flow, and functions. You'll learn how to write your own programs and how to work with Python's built-in functions and modules.

Once you have a good grasp of the basics, the book delves into more advanced topics. You'll learn about object-oriented programming, which is a programming paradigm that emphasizes objects, classes, and inheritance. You'll also learn about debugging and error handling, which are essential skills for any programmer. The book covers how to work with third-party libraries, which can save you time and effort when building your own applications.

In addition to covering general programming concepts, the book also covers specific applications of Python. You'll learn how to use Python for data analysis, using the Pandas and NumPy libraries. You'll also learn how to use Python for machine learning, using the Scikit-learn and TensorFlow libraries. Finally, you'll learn how to use Python for web development, using the Flask and Django frameworks.

Throughout the book, you'll find real-world examples and hands-on exercises that will help you solidify your knowledge and skills. You'll also learn best practices for writing efficient and maintainable code. By the end of the book, you'll be able to tackle any programming task with confidence.

"Python Mastery" is for anyone who wants to learn Python, from complete beginners to experienced programmers. Whether you're a student, a professional developer, or just someone who wants to learn how to code, this book has everything you need to become an expert in Python. So why wait? Let's get started on your journey to Python mastery today!

Python is a versatile and popular programming language that has gained immense popularity over the years, owing to its ease of use, readability, and a vast array of libraries and frameworks available. Today, Python has become the language of choice for many software developers, data scientists, and machine learning engineers worldwide.

Whether you're a complete beginner or an experienced programmer, "Python Mastery: The Complete Guide to Programming with Python" is a comprehensive guide that can take you from the basics of Python programming to expert-level proficiency. This book is designed to equip you with the knowledge and skills necessary to write efficient, maintainable, and scalable code that can handle any task.

The book begins with an introduction to Python, its history, and its applications. You'll learn about the different versions of Python and how to install Python on your computer. You'll also get a brief overview of the Python ecosystem, including the Python Package Index (PyPI), which is the official repository of third-party Python libraries and tools.

Once you have Python installed on your computer, the book will take you through the basics of programming, covering topics such as variables, data types, control flow, and functions. You'll learn how to write your own programs and how to work with Python's built-in functions and modules. The book also covers Python's object-oriented programming (OOP) paradigm, which is a powerful and flexible programming paradigm that emphasizes objects, classes, and inheritance.

As you progress through the book, you'll learn about more advanced topics such as debugging and error handling, which are essential skills for any programmer. You'll also learn how to work with third-party libraries, which can save you time and effort when building your own applications. The book covers the most popular libraries and frameworks for Python, such as NumPy, Pandas, Scikit-learn, TensorFlow, Flask, and Django.

In addition to covering general programming concepts, the book also covers specific applications of Python. You'll learn how to use Python for data analysis, using the Pandas and NumPy libraries. You'll also learn how to use Python for machine learning, using the Scikit-learn and TensorFlow libraries. Finally, you'll learn how to use Python for web development, using the Flask and Django frameworks.

Throughout the book, you'll find real-world examples and hands-on exercises that will help you solidify your knowledge and skills. You'll also learn best practices for writing efficient and maintainable code. By the end of the book, you'll be able to tackle any programming task with confidence.

"Python Mastery" is for anyone who wants to learn Python, from complete beginners to experienced programmers. The book is written in a clear and concise language that is easy to understand, making it an excellent resource for self-learners. Additionally, the book's structure and organization make it a great reference for professionals who need to use Python for their work.

Overall, "Python Mastery: The Complete Guide to Programming with Python" is an essential guide for anyone who wants to learn Python and become an expert programmer. With its comprehensive coverage of Python programming, data analysis, machine learning, and web development, this book is the ultimate resource for anyone who wants to unlock the full potential of Python.

Chapter 1: Installation and Setup

Python is a high-level, general-purpose programming language that is widely used by developers and data scientists for a wide range of applications. It is popular because of its simplicity, ease of use, and powerful features. In this chapter, we will guide you through the process of installing Python on your system and setting up a development environment.

1.1 Python Versions

Python has two major versions: Python 2.x and Python 3.x. Python 2.x was first released in 2000 and has been widely used for many years. However, the latest version of Python is Python 3.x, which was released in 2008. Python 2.x and Python 3.x are not compatible with each other, so it's important to choose the right version when installing Python.

For this book, we will focus on Python 3.x, specifically Python 3.6 or later. Python 3.x has many advantages over Python 2.x, including improved Unicode support, better memory management, and enhanced security features.

1.2 Installing Python on Windows

The easiest way to install Python on a Windows system is to download and run the Python installer from the official Python website. Follow these steps to install Python on a Windows system:

Step 1: Go to the official Python website at www.python.org/downloads/ and click on the "Download Python" button.

Step 2: On the download page, choose the latest version of Python 3.x for your system. For Windows, you can choose either the 32-bit or 64-bit version, depending on your system configuration.

Step 3: Once the download is complete, double-click on the

downloaded file to start the installation process.

Step 4: In the installation wizard, select the "Add Python 3.x to PATH" option to add Python to your system's environment variables. This will allow you to use Python from the command prompt.

Step 5: Follow the rest of the installation wizard to complete the installation. Once the installation is complete, you can verify that Python is installed correctly by opening a command prompt and typing "python" without the quotes. This should open the Python interpreter, which you can use to run Python programs.

1.3 Installing Python on Mac

Mac OS X comes with Python pre-installed. However, the version of Python that comes with Mac OS X may not be the latest version, and you may want to install a newer version of Python. Follow these steps to install Python on a Mac:

Step 1: Go to the official Python website at www.python.org/downloads/ and click on the "Download Python" button.

Step 2: On the download page, choose the latest version of Python 3.x for your system. For Mac, you can choose either the 64-bit or the

32-bit version, depending on your system configuration.

Step 3: Once the download is complete, double-click on the downloaded file to start the installation process.

Step 4: In the installation wizard, select the "Add Python 3.x to PATH" option to add Python to your system's environment variables. This will allow you to use Python from the command prompt.

Step 5: Follow the rest of the installation wizard to complete the installation. Once the installation is complete, you can verify that Python is installed correctly by opening a terminal window and typing "python3" without the quotes. This should open the Python interpreter, which you can use to run Python programs.

1.4 Installing Python on Linux

Most Linux distributions come with Python pre-installed. However, the version of Python that comes with your Linux distribution may not be the latest version, and you may want to install a newer version of Python. Follow these steps to install Python on.

Chapter 2: Basic Programming Concepts: Variables, Data Types, and Operators

In Chapter 1, we discussed the fundamental concepts of programming and the essential components of a programming language. Now, we will dive deeper into some of the fundamental programming concepts that are crucial for every programmer to understand. In this chapter, we will cover variables, data types, and operators.

2.1 Variables

A variable is a named storage location in a computer's memory that holds a value that can be changed during the program's execution. In other words, it is a container that holds a value, which can be modified by the program as it runs. Variables are essential in programming because they allow us to store data, manipulate it, and use it to make decisions and perform calculations.

To declare a variable in most programming languages, you must specify the variable's name and its data type. For example, in Java, you can declare an integer variable like this:

```
int x;
```
This line of code declares a variable called "x" of type integer. The integer data type is used to store whole numbers, such as 1, 2, 3, and so on. Once you have declared a variable, you can assign a value to it like this:

```
x = 10;
```
This line of code assigns the value 10 to the variable "x." Now, you can use the variable "x" in your program to perform calculations or make decisions.

2.2 Data Types

Data types are used to specify the type of data that a variable can hold. In programming, there are several data types, each with its own set of values and operations. The most common data types include integers, floating-point numbers, characters, and strings.

Integers are used to store whole numbers, such as 1, 2, 3, and so on. They can be signed or unsigned, depending on whether they can represent negative values or not. Floating-point numbers, also known as real numbers, are used to represent decimal numbers, such as 3.14 or 2.5. Characters are used to represent individual letters, numbers, and symbols, while strings are used to represent sequences of characters.

In addition to these basic data types, most programming languages also provide more complex data types, such as arrays, structures, and classes. These data types allow programmers to organize and manipulate data in more complex ways.

2.3 Operators

Operators are symbols or keywords that are used to perform operations on data. There are several types of operators in programming, including arithmetic operators, comparison operators, logical operators, and bitwise operators.

Arithmetic operators are used to perform mathematical operations, such as addition, subtraction, multiplication, and division. For example, the following code adds two integers:

```
int x = 10;
int y = 20;
int z = x + y;
```
In this code, the variable "z" is

assigned the value 30, which is the result of adding the values of "x" and "y."

Comparison operators are used to compare values and return a boolean value (true or false). For example, the following code compares two integers:

```
int x = 10;
int y = 20;
boolean result = x < y;
```
In this code, the variable "result" is assigned the value true because the value of "x" is less than the value of "y."

Logical operators are used to perform logical operations, such as AND, OR, and NOT. For example, the following code uses the AND operator:

```
boolean x = true;
boolean y = false;
boolean result = x && y;
```
In this code, the variable "result" is

Sure, let's expand on each of these concepts in more detail.

2.1 Variables

Variables are used to store values that can be used and manipulated throughout a program. They are typically declared with a specific data type, which determines the range of values that the variable can hold. In most programming languages, variables must be declared before they are used, and they can be assigned a value using the assignment operator (=).

For example, in Java, you can declare an integer variable like this:

int x;
This line of code declares a variable called "x" of type integer. The integer data type is used to store whole numbers, such as 1, 2, 3, and so on. Once you have declared a variable, you can assign a value to it like this:

x = 10;
This line of code assigns the value 10 to the variable "x." Now, you can use the variable "x" in your program to perform calculations or make decisions.

In addition to simple variables, many programming languages also provide more complex data structures that can hold multiple values, such as arrays and lists. These data structures can be used to store and manipulate larger amounts of data in a more organized way.

2.2 Data Types

Data types are used to specify the type of data that a variable can hold. In programming, there are several data types, each with its own set of values and operations. The most common data types include integers, floating-point numbers, characters, and strings.

Integers are used to store whole numbers, such as 1, 2, 3, and so on. They can be signed or unsigned, depending on whether they can represent negative values or not. Floating-point numbers, also known as real numbers, are used to represent decimal numbers, such as 3.14 or 2.5. Characters are used to represent individual letters, numbers, and symbols, while strings are used to represent sequences of characters.

In addition to these basic data types, most programming languages also provide more complex data types, such as arrays, structures, and classes. These data types allow programmers to organize and manipulate data in more complex ways.

Arrays are used to store a collection of values of the same data type. For example, an array of integers might look like this:

```
int[] myArray = {1, 2, 3, 4, 5};
```
This line of code declares an array called "myArray" that contains five integers. The array can be accessed using an index, which specifies the position of the value within the array.

Structures and classes are used to define custom data types that can hold multiple values of different data types. They can also include functions or methods that can be used to manipulate the data. For example, a class representing a person might include fields for the person's name, age, and address, as well as methods for updating or retrieving that information.

2.3 Operators

Operators are symbols or keywords that are used to perform operations on data. There are several types of operators in programming, including arithmetic operators, comparison operators, logical operators, and bitwise operators.

Arithmetic operators are used to perform mathematical operations, such as addition, subtraction, multiplication, and division. For example, the following code adds two integers:

```
int x = 10;
int y = 20;
int z = x + y;
```

In this code, the variable "z" is assigned the value 30, which is the result of adding the values of "x" and "y."

Comparison operators are used to compare values and return a boolean value (true or false). For example, the following code compares two integers:

2.3.1 Arithmetic Operators

Arithmetic operators are used to perform mathematical operations on numerical data types. The most common arithmetic operators are:

Addition (+): adds two values together.
Subtraction (-): subtracts one value from another.
Multiplication (*): multiplies two values together.
Division (/): divides one value by another.
Modulus (%): returns the remainder after division.
For example, consider the following code:

```
int x = 5;
int y = 3;
int z = x + y;
int a = x * y;
int b = x / y;
```

```
int c = x % y;
```
The variable "z" would be assigned the value 8, which is the result of adding "x" and "y." The variable "a" would be assigned the value 15, which is the result of multiplying "x" and "y." The variable "b" would be assigned the value 1, which is the result of dividing "x" by "y" (note that integer division truncates any decimal part of the result). Finally, the variable "c" would be assigned the value 2, which is the remainder of dividing "x" by "y."

2.3.2 Comparison Operators

Comparison operators are used to compare two values and return a boolean value (true or false) based on the result of the comparison.

The most common comparison operators are:

Equal to (==): returns true if two values are equal.
Not equal to (!=): returns true if two values are not equal.
Greater than (>): returns true if one value is greater than another.
Greater than or equal to (>=): returns true if one value is greater than or equal to another.
Less than (<): returns true if one value is less than another.
Less than or equal to (<=): returns true if one value is less than or equal to another.
For example, consider the following code:

```
int x = 5;
int y = 3;
boolean a = x == y;
boolean b = x != y;
boolean c = x > y;
boolean d = x >= y;
boolean e = x < y;
boolean f = x <= y;
```

The variable "a" would be assigned the value false, since "x" and "y" are not equal. The variable "b" would be assigned the value true, since "x" and "y" are not equal. The variable "c" would be assigned the value true, since "x" is greater than "y." The variable "d" would be assigned the value true, since "x" is greater than or equal to "y." The variable "e" would be assigned the value false, since "x" is not less than "y." Finally, the variable "f" would be assigned the value false, since "x" is not less than or equal to "y."

2.3.3 Logical Operators

Logical operators are used to combine two or more boolean values and return a boolean value based on the result of the combination. The most common logical operators are:

And (&&): returns true if both values are true.
Or (||): returns true if either value is true.
Not (!): returns the opposite of a boolean value.
For example, consider the following code:

```
boolean x = true;
boolean y = false;
boolean a = x && y;
boolean b = x || y;
boolean c = !x;
```
The variable "a" would be assigned the value false, since both "x" and "y" are

Chapter 3: Conditional Statements and Loops

In programming, we often need to execute certain blocks of code based on certain conditions. We can achieve this using conditional statements and loops. In this chapter, we will discuss conditional statements and loops in detail.

Conditional Statements

Conditional statements are used to execute specific blocks of code based on certain conditions. In Python, we have the following conditional statements:

if statement
if-else statement
if-elif-else statement
nested if statements
if Statement

The if statement is used to execute a block of code if a certain condition is true. The syntax for the if statement is as follows:

```
if condition:
    statement1
    statement2
```

statement3

...

Here, condition is the expression that is evaluated to True or False. If the condition is True, then the statements inside the block are executed. If the condition is False, then the statements inside the block are skipped.

For example:

```
x = 5

if x > 3:
    print("x is greater than 3")
```
In this example, the condition x > 3 is True, so the statement "x is greater than 3" is printed.

if-else Statement

The if-else statement is used to execute one block of code if the condition is true, and another block of code if the condition is false. The syntax for the if-else statement is as follows:

```
if condition:
    statement1
    statement2
    statement3
    ...
else:
    statement4
    statement5
    statement6
    ...
```

Here, if the condition is True, the statements inside the if block are executed, and if the condition is

False, the statements inside the else block are executed.

For example:

```
x = 2

if x > 3:
    print("x is greater than 3")
else:
    print("x is less than or equal to 3")
```

In this example, the condition x > 3 is False, so the statement "x is less than or equal to 3" is printed.

if-elif-else Statement

The if-elif-else statement is used to execute different blocks of code based on multiple conditions. The syntax for the if-elif-else statement is as follows:

```
if condition1:
    statement1
    statement2
    statement3
    ...
elif condition2:
    statement4
    statement5
    statement6
    ...
elif condition3:
    statement7
    statement8
    statement9
    ...
else:
    statement10
    statement11
```

statement12
...
Here, the conditions are checked one by one, and if a condition is True, the corresponding block of statements is executed. If none of the conditions are True, then the statements inside the else block are executed.

For example:

bash
Copy code

```
x = 10

if x < 0:
    print("x is negative")
elif x == 0:
    print("x is zero")
else:
```

```
    print("x is positive")
```
In this example, the condition x < 0 is False, and the condition x == 0 is also False, so the statement "x is positive" is printed.

Nested if Statements

Nested if statements are if statements that are nested inside other if statements. This allows us to check for multiple conditions. The syntax for nested if statements is as follows:

yaml
Copy code
```
if condition1:
    if condition2:
        statement1
        statement2
```

```
    statement3
    ...
else:
    statement4
```

Chapter 4: Data Structures: Lists, Tuples, Sets, and Dictionaries

In this chapter, we will explore the four most commonly used data structures in Python: lists, tuples, sets, and dictionaries. These data structures are essential in almost all Python programs, and they are used to store, organize, and manipulate data efficiently.

4.1 Lists

A list is an ordered sequence of values. It is defined using square brackets ([]), and the values are separated by commas. Lists are mutable, meaning that we can add, delete, or modify elements in a list. We can access the elements of a list using indexing, where the first element has an index of 0.

Here's an example of a list in Python:

python

fruits = ['apple', 'banana', 'cherry']
In this example, the list contains three elements, 'apple', 'banana', and 'cherry'. We can access each element using indexing:

python

```python
print(fruits[0])  # Output: 'apple'
print(fruits[1])  # Output: 'banana'
print(fruits[2])  # Output: 'cherry'
```

We can also modify the elements of a list:

python

```python
fruits[1] = 'orange'
print(fruits)  # Output: ['apple', 'orange', 'cherry']
```

Lists also have several built-in methods that allow us to manipulate them. Here are a few examples:

python

```python
fruits.append('grape')  # Add an element to the end of the list
print(fruits)  # Output: ['apple', 'orange', 'cherry', 'grape']
```

```python
fruits.insert(1, 'kiwi')  # Insert an
element at a specific index
print(fruits)  # Output: ['apple', 'kiwi',
'orange', 'cherry', 'grape']

fruits.remove('cherry')  # Remove a
specific element
print(fruits)  # Output: ['apple', 'kiwi',
'orange', 'grape']

fruits.sort()  # Sort the elements of
the list
print(fruits)  # Output: ['apple',
'grape', 'kiwi', 'orange']
```

4.2 Tuples

A tuple is an ordered sequence of
values, similar to a list. However,
tuples are immutable, meaning that
we cannot add, delete, or modify
elements in a tuple. Tuples are

defined using parentheses (()), and the values are separated by commas.

Here's an example of a tuple in Python:

python

```
coordinates = (3, 4)
```

In this example, the tuple contains two elements, 3 and 4. We can access each element using indexing:

python

```
print(coordinates[0])  # Output: 3
print(coordinates[1])  # Output: 4
```

We cannot modify the elements of a tuple:

python

```python
coordinates[0] = 5  # This will result in a TypeError
```

However, we can create a new tuple by concatenating two or more tuples:

python

```python
coordinates2 = (5, 6)
new_coordinates = coordinates + coordinates2
print(new_coordinates)  # Output: (3, 4, 5, 6)
```

4.3 Sets

A set is an unordered collection of unique elements. Sets are defined using curly braces ({}) or the set() function. Sets are mutable, meaning that we can add or remove elements from a set.

Here's an example of a set in Python:

python

```
my_set = {1, 2, 3, 4}
```
In this example

Chapter 5: Input and Output: Reading and Writing Files in Python

In Python, file input and output operations are crucial for working with data. Whether it's reading data from a file or writing data to a file,

file operations are an essential part of any data analysis or processing task. In this chapter, we will discuss how to read and write files in Python.

5.1 Opening Files

Before we can read or write files in Python, we need to open them first. To open a file, we use the open() function, which takes two arguments - the file name and the mode in which we want to open the file. The mode can be one of the following:

'r': read mode
'w': write mode
'a': append mode
'x': exclusive mode

'b': binary mode
't': text mode
'+': read and write mode
Let's take a look at how we can
open a file in read mode:

kotlin

file = open('filename.txt', 'r')
In the above code, we are opening
a file called filename.txt in read
mode. If the file is not present in
the current directory, Python will
raise a FileNotFoundError. We can
also specify the file path if the file
is located in a different directory:

kotlin

file = open('/path/to/filename.txt',
'r')
Once we are done reading or

writing to the file, we should close the file using the close() method:

```go
go
```

```
file.close()
```
If we forget to close the file, Python will close it automatically when the program ends, but it's a good practice to close the file explicitly.

5.2 Reading Files

Once we have opened a file in read mode, we can read its contents using various methods. The most basic method is read(), which reads the entire contents of the file and returns it as a string:

```lua
lua
```

```
file = open('filename.txt', 'r')
contents = file.read()
file.close()
```

In the above code, we are reading the entire contents of filename.txt and storing it in the contents variable. We can also specify how many bytes we want to read using the read(n) method, where n is the number of bytes to be read:

lua

```
file = open('filename.txt', 'r')
contents = file.read(10)  # read first 10 bytes
file.close()
```

We can also read a file line by line using the readline() method:

scss

```
file = open('filename.txt', 'r')
line = file.readline()
while line:
    print(line)
    line = file.readline()
file.close()
```

In the above code, we are reading each line of filename.txt and printing it to the console. We can also read all the lines of a file at once using the readlines() method:

lua

```
file = open('filename.txt', 'r')
lines = file.readlines()
for line in lines:
    print(line)
file.close()
```

5.3 Writing Files

To write data to a file in Python, we need to open the file in write or append mode. In write mode, if the file already exists, it will be overwritten, whereas in append mode, the data will be added to the end of the file. Let's take a look at how we can write data to a file:

lua

```
file = open('filename.txt', 'w')
file.write('Hello, world!')
file.close()
```
In the above code, we are writing the string 'Hello, world!' to filename.txt. If the file

Chapter 6: Inheritance and Polymorphism

In the previous chapters, we have learned about classes and objects, and how they are used to model real-world entities in software applications. In this chapter, we will explore the concepts of inheritance and polymorphism, which are powerful tools for organizing and reusing code.

6.1 Inheritance

Inheritance is a fundamental concept in object-oriented programming. It is a mechanism that allows one class to inherit properties and behavior from another class. The class that inherits from another class is called the subclass, and the class that is inherited from is called the superclass.

To demonstrate inheritance, let us consider an example. Suppose we have a superclass called Person that contains properties such as name, age, and gender. We can create a subclass called Employee that inherits from Person and adds additional properties such as salary, job_title, and hire_date. The Employee class can access the properties of the Person class as well as its own properties.

Inheritance is implemented in Python using the class statement followed by the name of the subclass, and the name of the superclass in parentheses. For example, to create the Employee subclass that inherits from Person, we would write:

python

```python
class Employee(Person):
    def __init__(self, name, age, gender, salary, job_title, hire_date):
        super().__init__(name, age, gender)
        self.salary = salary
        self.job_title = job_title
        self.hire_date = hire_date
```

In this example, we have defined an __init__ method that initializes the properties of the Employee class, as well as calls the __init__ method of the Person class using the super() function.

In addition to inheriting properties, a subclass can also inherit methods from its superclass. For example, suppose the Person class had a method called get_age that returns the age of the person. The Employee class can inherit this method and use it in its own methods. To do this, we would write:

python

```python
class Employee(Person):
    def __init__(self, name, age, gender, salary, job_title, hire_date):
        super().__init__(name, age, gender)
```

```python
        self.salary = salary
        self.job_title = job_title
        self.hire_date = hire_date

    def get_years_of_service(self):
        today = date.today()
        return today.year -
self.hire_date.year

    def get_salary(self):
        return self.salary

    def get_age(self):
        return super().get_age()  # call
the get_age method of the Person
class
```
In this example, we have defined
three methods in the Employee
class: get_years_of_service,
get_salary, and get_age. The
get_years_of_service method

calculates the number of years the employee has been working based on the hire_date property. The get_salary method returns the salary of the employee. The get_age method calls the get_age method of the Person class using the super() function, which returns the age of the employee.

Inheritance can be used to create a hierarchy of classes, where each subclass inherits from its superclass, and can add its own properties and behavior. This allows us to reuse code and avoid duplication, making our programs more efficient and easier to maintain.

6.2 Polymorphism

Polymorphism is another important concept in object-oriented programming. It allows us to use objects of different classes in the same way, by treating them as instances of a common superclass. This is achieved through the

Chapter 7: Advanced Debugging Techniques

In the previous chapters, we covered basic debugging techniques and how to handle errors effectively. However, there are times when basic debugging techniques are not enough, and more advanced techniques are required. In this chapter, we will cover some advanced debugging techniques that can help you troubleshoot code more effectively.

Debugging Tools
There are several debugging tools that can help you identify and resolve issues in your code. These tools can automate the debugging process and reduce the time and effort required to identify and resolve errors.

One of the most popular debugging tools is a debugger. A debugger is a software tool that allows you to step through your code line by line and inspect the values of variables and expressions at each step. This can help you identify the exact line of code that is causing an error and understand the state of your code at that point.

Another useful tool is a profiler. A profiler is a tool that measures the performance of your code and identifies bottlenecks that may be causing slow execution. Profilers can help you optimize your code and improve its performance.

Finally, there are many code analysis tools available that can help you identify potential issues in your code. These tools can check for common coding mistakes, such as syntax errors and logical errors, and suggest ways to improve your code.

Advanced Debugging Techniques
In addition to using debugging
tools, there are several advanced
debugging techniques that can
help you identify and resolve issues
in your code. Here are a few
techniques you can use:

a. Divide and Conquer

When you encounter a bug in your
code, it can be overwhelming to try
to identify the cause of the
problem. A useful technique is to
divide the problem into smaller
parts and tackle each part
individually.

For example, if you have a function
that is not working properly, you
can try to isolate the problem by

breaking the function into smaller functions and testing each one individually. This can help you identify the exact part of the function that is causing the error.

b. Reverse Engineering

Another useful technique is to reverse engineer your code. This involves working backwards from the error to identify the cause of the problem.

For example, if you have a runtime error, you can start by examining the stack trace to identify the function that caused the error. Then, you can examine the code in that function to identify the specific line of code that caused the error.

c. Rubber Duck Debugging

Sometimes, simply talking through your code with someone else can help you identify the cause of a problem. Rubber duck debugging involves explaining your code to a rubber duck or other inanimate object.

By explaining your code out loud, you may identify mistakes or logical errors that you would not have noticed otherwise. This technique can be especially useful when you are stuck on a difficult problem and need to think creatively.

d. Logging

Logging is a technique that involves adding messages to your code that indicate the state of your code at different points in the execution process. These messages can help you understand what is happening in your code and identify the cause of a problem.

For example, you can add logging messages to a function to indicate the values of variables at different points in the function. This can help you identify when a variable is being set incorrectly or when a loop is not executing as expected.

Best Practices
In addition to using debugging tools and techniques, there are several best practices that can help

you avoid bugs and handle errors effectively. Here are a few best practices to follow:

a. Test Your Code

One of the most effective ways to avoid bugs is to test your code thoroughly. This involves writing test cases that cover different scenarios and executing those tests to ensure that your code works as expected.

b. Use Version Control

Version control is a technique that involves tracking changes to your code over

Chapter 8: Modules and Libraries: Working with Third-Party Packages

In the world of programming, no developer can survive without using third-party packages or libraries. These packages are pre-written code that programmers can use in their projects to save time and effort. In this chapter, we will explore how to work with third-party packages, including installing, importing, and using them in our projects.

8.1 Introduction to Third-Party Packages

Third-party packages are libraries or modules that are not part of the core Python language. These packages are created by other developers and are made available for use by anyone. They are designed to solve specific problems or provide functionality that is not available in the core Python language.

The Python Package Index (PyPI) is the largest repository of third-party packages for the Python programming language. PyPI has thousands of packages that can be installed using pip, the Python package manager. Pip is a command-line tool that allows developers to install, update, and uninstall packages.

8.2 Installing Third-Party Packages

Before we can use a third-party package in our project, we need to install it. Installing a package is easy, thanks to pip. To install a package, we need to open the command prompt or terminal and type the following command:

go

pip install <package-name>
For example, to install the NumPy package, we can run the following command:

pip install numpy
This will download and install the NumPy package on our computer. We only need to install a package once, and it will be available for use in all our Python projects.

8.3 Importing Third-Party Packages

Once we have installed a package, we can import it into our Python code. To import a package, we use the import keyword followed by the package name. For example, to import the NumPy package, we can use the following code:

python

```
import numpy
```

This code will make all the functions and classes in the NumPy package available for use in our Python code. We can also use an alias when importing a package, using the as keyword. For example, to import NumPy with an alias np, we can use the following code:

python

```python
import numpy as np
```

This code will make all the functions and classes in the NumPy package available for use, but we will have to use the np alias instead of numpy when calling these functions and classes.

8.4 Using Third-Party Packages

Once we have imported a package, we can use its functions and classes in our Python code. For example, let's say we want to use the numpy.array function to create a NumPy array. We can use the following code:

python

```python
import numpy as np

arr = np.array([1, 2, 3])
print(arr)
```

This code will create a NumPy array with the values [1, 2, 3] and print it to the console.

8.5 Updating and Uninstalling Packages

Over time, packages may receive updates to fix bugs, add new features, or improve performance. To update a package, we can use the following command:

css

pip install --upgrade <package-name>

For example, to update the NumPy package, we can use the following command:

css

pip install --upgrade numpy

This will download and install the latest version of the NumPy package.

If we no longer need a package, we can uninstall it using the following command:

go

pip uninstall <package-name>

For example, to uninstall the

NumPy package, we can use the following command:

```
pip uninstall numpy
```
This will

Chapter 9: Advanced Techniques in Data Analysis with Pandas and NumPy Libraries

In this chapter, we will dive deeper into the advanced techniques in data analysis using the Pandas and NumPy libraries. We will explore how to deal with missing data, how to merge datasets, and how to handle large datasets.

9.1 Dealing with Missing Data

Missing data is a common problem in data analysis. It can occur due to various reasons such as data entry errors, data corruption, or missing values in the original dataset. The Pandas library provides several tools to deal with missing data.

The first step in dealing with missing data is to identify the missing values. We can use the isnull() method to check for missing values in a DataFrame. This method returns a boolean DataFrame that shows True where there is a missing value and False otherwise.

python

```python
import pandas as pd
import numpy as np

# Create a sample DataFrame with
missing values
df = pd.DataFrame({'A': [1, 2,
np.nan, 4],
            'B': [5, np.nan, np.nan, 8],
            'C': [9, 10, 11, 12]})

# Check for missing values
print(df.isnull())
Output:
```

mathematica

```
     A     B     C
0  False False False
1  False  True False
2   True  True False
3  False False False
```
Once we have identified the

missing values, we can either drop them or fill them with appropriate values. The dropna() method can be used to drop the rows or columns that contain missing values. The dropna() method has several parameters that allow us to control the behavior of the method.

sql

```
# Drop rows with missing values
df.dropna()
```

```
# Drop columns with missing
values
df.dropna(axis=1)
```

```
# Drop rows where all values are
missing
df.dropna(how='all')
```

```python
# Drop rows where at least 2
values are missing
df.dropna(thresh=2)

# Drop rows where missing values
are in a specific column
df.dropna(subset=['B'])
```

We can also fill the missing values with appropriate values using the fillna() method. The fillna() method can take a scalar value, a dictionary, or a Series to fill the missing values.

sql

```python
# Fill missing values with a scalar
value
df.fillna(0)

# Fill missing values with the mean
of the column
```

```python
df.fillna(df.mean())

# Fill missing values with a
dictionary
df.fillna({'A': 0, 'B': 1})

# Fill missing values with a forward
fill
df.fillna(method='ffill')

# Fill missing values with a
backward fill
df.fillna(method='bfill')
```
9.2 Merging Datasets

Merging datasets is a common operation in data analysis. The Pandas library provides several methods to merge datasets based on common columns.

We will use the merge() method to merge two datasets based on common columns. The merge() method has several parameters that allow us to control the behavior of the method.

bash

```
# Create two sample DataFrames
to merge
df1 = pd.DataFrame({'key': ['A', 'B',
'C', 'D'],
            'value': [1, 2, 3, 4]})
df2 = pd.DataFrame({'key': ['B', 'D',
'E', 'F'],
            'value': [5, 6, 7, 8]})

# Merge the two DataFrames
merged_df = pd.merge(df1, df2,
on='key')
```

The above code will merge the two DataFrames based on the

Chapter 10: Deep Learning with TensorFlow

In the previous chapter, we discussed various machine learning algorithms and their implementation using the scikit-learn library. However, these algorithms have certain limitations when it comes to solving complex problems such as image recognition, natural language processing, and speech recognition. In such cases, deep learning algorithms come to the rescue.

Deep learning is a subfield of machine learning that uses artificial neural networks to learn from large amounts of data. Deep learning algorithms can automatically extract features from data and use them to make predictions or classify new data. Deep learning has been applied to a wide range of applications such as image recognition, natural language processing, speech recognition, and autonomous driving.

In this chapter, we will introduce the TensorFlow library, which is one of the most popular libraries for deep learning. We will cover the basics of TensorFlow and demonstrate how to build and train deep neural networks using TensorFlow.

Introduction to TensorFlow

TensorFlow is an open-source library for numerical computation and machine learning. It was developed by the Google Brain team and was released under the Apache 2.0 open source license in 2015. TensorFlow is written in C++ and provides a Python API for easy use. It is designed to be scalable and can run on multiple CPUs and GPUs.

TensorFlow uses a computational graph to represent the mathematical operations performed by the neural network. The graph consists of nodes and edges, where the nodes represent the operations and the edges represent the data flow between the nodes. The computational graph is built using TensorFlow's API, and the graph is then executed using a TensorFlow session.

TensorFlow provides various modules for building deep neural networks, including:

tf.keras: A high-level API for building neural networks.
tf.nn: A low-level API for building neural networks.
tf.estimator: A high-level API for building pre-made models.
Building a Neural Network with TensorFlow
To demonstrate how to build a

neural network using TensorFlow, we will use the MNIST dataset, which is a dataset of handwritten digits. The dataset consists of 60,000 training images and 10,000 test images.

Loading the Dataset
To load the MNIST dataset, we will use the keras module, which is a high-level API for building neural networks in TensorFlow.

makefile

```
from tensorflow import keras

# Load the MNIST dataset
mnist = keras.datasets.mnist

# Split the dataset into training and
testing sets
```

```
(train_images, train_labels),
(test_images, test_labels) =
mnist.load_data()
```

```
# Normalize the pixel values
between 0 and 1
train_images = train_images /
255.0
test_images = test_images / 255.0
```

The load_data() function returns
two tuples, one containing the
training images and labels, and the
other containing the test images
and labels. We then normalize the
pixel values between 0 and 1 by
dividing each pixel value by 255.

Building the Model
To build the neural network, we will
use the keras.Sequential class,
which allows us to build a model

layer by layer. We will use three layers: a flatten layer, a dense layer with 128 neurons and a ReLU activation function, and a dense layer with 10 neurons and a softmax activation function.

python

```python
from tensorflow.keras import Sequential
from tensorflow.keras.layers import Flatten, Dense

# Build the model
model = Sequential([
    Flatten(input_shape=(28, 28)),
    Dense(128, activation='relu'),
    Dense(10, activation='softmax')
])
```

The first layer, Flatten, transforms

the 28x28 image into a 1D array of length 784. The second layer, Dense, has 128 neurons and uses the ReLU activation function. The last layer, Dense, has

Chapter 11: Scaling Your Web Application with Flask and Django

Web development is a dynamic and constantly evolving field. As your web application grows and attracts more users, you need to ensure that it can handle increased traffic and maintain its performance. This is where scaling comes in. In this chapter, we will explore the various techniques and strategies for scaling your web application using Flask and Django frameworks.

1: Vertical Scaling

Vertical scaling involves increasing the resources of a single server, such as CPU, RAM, and storage capacity, to improve its performance. This is the easiest and quickest way to scale your web application. Flask and Django both support vertical scaling.

In Flask, you can use the built-in development server for testing and development purposes. However, it is not recommended for production use. Instead, you should use a web server, such as Apache or Nginx, to serve your Flask application. These web servers can handle multiple requests and can be configured to optimize the performance of your application.

In Django, you can also use a web server, such as Apache or Nginx, to serve your application. Additionally, Django supports the use of caching to improve performance. Django includes a built-in caching framework that supports caching data in memory, on disk, or in a distributed cache like Memcached or Redis.

2: Horizontal Scaling
Horizontal scaling involves adding more servers to handle increased traffic and distribute the load across multiple machines. This approach requires more effort and resources than vertical scaling, but it can handle larger amounts of traffic and provide better performance. Flask and Django

both support horizontal scaling. In Flask, you can use a load balancer, such as HAProxy or Nginx, to distribute incoming requests across multiple Flask instances running on different servers. Each Flask instance can communicate with a centralized database to retrieve and store data. Additionally, Flask supports the use of task queues, such as Celery, to offload long-running tasks to separate worker processes.

In Django, you can use a load balancer, such as HAProxy or Nginx, to distribute incoming requests across multiple Django instances running on different servers. Django supports the use of a database connection pool to handle multiple database connections and improve performance. Additionally, Django supports the use of task queues, such as Celery, to offload long-running tasks to separate worker processes.

3: Database Scaling
Database scaling involves optimizing your database to handle increased traffic and improve performance. Flask and Django both support database scaling.
In Flask, you can use a database connection pool to handle multiple database connections and improve performance. Additionally, Flask supports the use of database sharding, which involves splitting a single database into multiple

smaller databases to distribute the load across multiple machines.

In Django, you can use a database connection pool to handle multiple database connections and improve performance. Additionally, Django supports the use of database sharding and replication, which involves replicating data across multiple databases to improve availability and distribute the load across multiple machines.

4: Caching
Caching involves storing frequently accessed data in memory or on disk to improve performance. Flask and Django both support caching. In Flask, you can use the Flask-Caching extension to cache data in

memory, on disk, or in a distributed cache like Memcached or Redis. Additionally, Flask supports the use of HTTP caching, which involves caching responses in the user's browser or in a proxy server to reduce the number of requests to the server.

In Django, you can use the built-in caching framework to cache data in memory, on disk, or in a distributed cache like Memcached or Redis. Additionally, Django supports the use of HTTP caching and template fragment caching, which involves caching parts of a template that are frequently accessed to reduce the number of requests to the server.

5: Content Delivery Network (CDN)
A Content Delivery Network

Chapter 12: Best Practices and
Tips: Writing Efficient and
Maintainable Code

As a software developer, writing
efficient and maintainable code is
one of the most important skills
you can possess. It can be the
difference between a project that
runs smoothly and one that is
plagued with bugs, slow
performance, and difficult
maintenance. In this chapter, we
will explore best practices and tips
for writing efficient and
maintainable code.

1: Keep Your Code Simple and Concise
The best code is simple and concise. Avoid over-engineering and unnecessary complexity. When you keep your code simple, it is easier to understand, maintain, and debug. Aim for clarity and readability. Avoid using too many conditional statements or loops. Consider breaking down complex problems into smaller, more manageable pieces.

2: Use Meaningful Names for Variables, Functions, and Classes
One of the most important aspects of writing maintainable code is using meaningful names for variables, functions, and classes. Use names that clearly describe

the purpose and functionality of each element. Avoid abbreviations and acronyms unless they are commonly understood in the domain of the project.

3: Write Modular and Reusable Code

Modular and reusable code is essential for efficient and maintainable code. By breaking down complex problems into smaller, reusable modules, you can reduce duplication, improve readability, and make it easier to maintain your code. Use a consistent naming convention for your modules, and make sure they are well documented.

4: Follow a Consistent Code Style and Formatting

Consistent code style and formatting make your code easier to read and understand. Use a consistent indentation style, brace placement, and naming convention. Consider using a code linter or formatter to enforce consistent formatting across your codebase.

5: Use Comments and Documentation

Comments and documentation are essential for maintaining code over time. Use comments to explain the purpose and functionality of your code. Document your functions, classes, and modules with clear and concise descriptions, input/output parameters, and examples.

6: Write Testable Code

Testable code is code that can be easily tested. By writing testable code, you can reduce the number of bugs and improve the quality of your code. Use dependency injection to decouple your code and make it easier to test. Write unit tests for your functions and modules, and consider using a test-driven development approach.

7: Avoid Magic Numbers and Hard-Coded Values

Magic numbers and hard-coded values can make your code difficult to understand and maintain. Instead, use named constants or configuration files to define these values. This makes it easier to change them later and avoids the need to search through your code for hard-coded values.

8: Use Error Handling and Logging
Error handling and logging are important for maintaining code over time. Use try-catch blocks to handle errors gracefully, and log error messages to a centralized location. This makes it easier to debug errors and identify issues with your code.

9: Use Source Control and Versioning
Source control and versioning are essential for managing code over time. Use a source control system

like Git to track changes to your code and collaborate with other developers. Use versioning to keep track of changes to your code over time.

10: Continuously Refactor and Improve Your Code
Finally, continuously refactor and improve your code over time. Identify areas of your code that can be improved and refactor them to make them more efficient and maintainable. Use code reviews to get feedback from other developers and identify areas of your code that can be improved.

In conclusion, writing efficient and maintainable code is essential for software developers. By following these best practices and tips, you can improve the quality of your code and make it easier to maintain over time. Remember to keep your code simple, use meaningful names, write modular and reusable code, follow a consistent code style,

Congratulations on completing "Python Mastery: The Complete Guide to Programming with Python from Beginner to Expert!" This book has taken you on a journey from the very basics of Python to advanced topics, equipping you with the knowledge and skills to become a proficient Python programmer.

Python is one of the most popular programming languages in the world, and for good reason. It is a powerful language that can be used for a wide range of tasks, from web development to data analysis, machine learning, and more. The language's ease of use, simplicity, and readability make it an ideal choice for both beginners and experienced developers alike.

Throughout this book, you have learned about the fundamental concepts of programming, such as variables, data types, loops, and functions, and how to apply them in Python. You have also explored advanced topics like object-oriented programming, algorithms, data structures, and more. With each chapter, you have gained a deeper understanding of the language and its capabilities, and you have become more confident in your ability to write efficient, effective Python code.

But this book is not just about learning the syntax and semantics of Python. It is also about developing good programming practices, such as code readability, modularity, and testing. These practices will help you write maintainable and scalable code, which is essential when working on larger projects or in teams.

As you continue on your journey as a Python programmer, remember that learning never stops. The

Python community is constantly evolving, and there are always new libraries, frameworks, and tools to explore. Embrace this continuous learning process, and stay curious and open-minded.

In conclusion, "Python Mastery: The Complete Guide to Programming with Python from Beginner to Expert" has provided you with a comprehensive understanding of Python programming. You are now equipped with the knowledge and skills to write efficient, effective, and maintainable code in Python. I hope this book has been a valuable resource in your journey as a programmer, and I wish you all the

best in your future endeavors.
Happy coding!